BABIES

Robyn Gee

Designed by Roger Priddy

Revision by Susan Meredith, Isaac Quaye and Susannah Owen

Illustrated by Sue Stitt,
David Gifford, Kuo Kang Chen and Lee Montgomery

Consultants: Judy Cunnington, Relate Marriage Guidance Council;
Fran Reader, Senior Registrar in Obstetrics and Gynaecology,
University College Hospital, London;
Judith Schott, SRN, Antenatal teacher trained by the National Childbirth Trust;
Dr Peter Hope, Research Registrar, Neonatal Unit,
University College Hospital, London.
Cover photograph courtesy of Lupe Cunha.

Contents

First published in 1985 by Usborne Publishing Ltd, Usborne House, 83-85 Saffron Hill, London EC1N 8RT, England. Copyright © 1985 Usborne Publishing Ltd. This edition copyright © 1997 Usborne Publishing Ltd. The name Usborne and the device ⏚ are Trade Marks of Usborne Publishing Ltd. All rights reserved. No part of this publication may be reproduced, stored in a retrieval system or transmitted in any form or by any means, electronic, mechanical, photocopying, recording or otherwise, without the prior permission of the publisher. Printed in Spain.

About this book

This book tells the fascinating story of how each new person arrives in the world. It describes how babies start and what happens to both a mother and her baby during pregnancy. It explains exactly what happens when a baby is born and gives you some idea of how a new baby may feel, look and behave. There is lots of information on how to help look after a baby, including some useful safety tips in the Babysitter's guide at the end of the book.

The key stages in a baby's development, up to the age of around two, are also included. This section may be of particular interest if someone you know is expecting a baby, or if you are thinking about a career which involves some aspect of pregnancy or childcare. If you want to find out more information than is included here, look at the Useful addresses section on page 47 for a list of organizations to get in touch with.

Most of the difficult words relating to pregnancy and birth are explained when they first appear, but if you come across any words that you do not understand, or you forget what they mean, try looking them up in the Glossary on page 47.

The colours used in the pictures of things inside the body are not true to life. Most of these things are also shown either much larger or much smaller than life-size but, where possible, an indication of the actual size has been given.

To avoid constantly repeating "the baby" or writing "he or she", we have used "he" in some places and "she" in others. When referring to an unborn baby, however, we have used "it", as people usually do this when they are talking.

From the moment a baby starts, even before it is the size of one of the commas on this page, it is a unique individual. When people talk about how babies grow and develop, they tend to talk about averages - the average weight and height at a particular age, the average time they spend sleeping, the average age at which they learn to do things. Perfectly normal babies, however, vary from these averages enormously and very few babies are average in all respects. Where averages are given, they are merely a guideline about what to expect if you know very little about babies.

How a baby starts

Each human being is made up of billions and billions of separate living units called cells. The story of how a new human being comes into existence begins with just two of these tiny cells - an egg cell and a sperm cell. Egg cells are produced inside the mother's body and sperm in the father's. A baby starts when an egg cell and a sperm meet and join together to form one new cell. The moment when the egg and sperm join is called conception or fertilization.

Egg cells

I An egg cell is also called an ovum. (The plural of ovum is ova.) When a baby girl is born, she already has about 400,000 ova stored inside her body in two ovaries. When she grows up, an ovum ripens each month in one of her ovaries and is released. This is called ovulation.

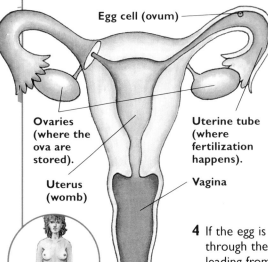

Egg cell (ovum)

Ovaries (where the ova are stored).

Uterine tube (where fertilization happens).

Uterus (womb)

Vagina

2

The ovum is released from the ovary into a tube called a uterine or Fallopian tube. If it meets a sperm while it is in the tube, it may be joined, or fertilized, by the sperm.

3

From the uterine tube the ovum travels into the womb or uterus. This is a hollow bag made of muscle, with a thick, soft lining of blood vessels. If the ovum is fertilized, it can embed itself in the lining of the uterus and start to grow.

4 If the egg is not fertilized, it passes through the vagina. This is a stretchy tube leading from the uterus to the outside of a woman's body.

Sperm

Sperm are tiny tadpole-shaped cells, which are produced and stored inside a man's testicles (also called testes). They are made in great quantities, about 200 million or more maturing each day. The testicles hang outside a man's body in a loose pouch of skin called the scrotum. There is a tube down the middle of the penis which carries urine from the bladder out of the body. The testicles are connected to this by tubes called sperm ducts.

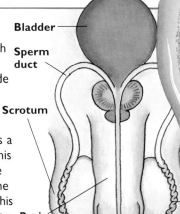

Bladder

Sperm duct

Scrotum

Testicles (testes)

Penis

The journey of the sperm

1 When a man and a woman have sexual intercourse, a man's penis fits into a woman's vagina. At the climax of intercourse for the man (male orgasm), the sperm travel from their storage place in the testicles through the sperm ducts to the penis.

2 As the sperm travel through the ducts, fluids are added to them to produce a mixture called semen. During the orgasm the semen is squirted out (ejaculated) from the penis into the woman's vagina.

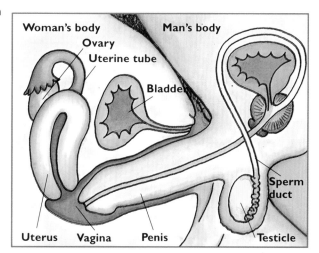

Woman's body
Ovary
Uterine tube
Man's body
Bladder
Uterus   Vagina   Penis
Sperm duct
Testicle

3 From the vagina the sperm swim up into the uterus and from there to the uterine tubes. One ejaculation contains about 300 million sperm, but only about 1,000 get as far as the tubes before they die.

4 If the sperm meet an ovum in one of the uterine tubes, they all cluster around it and try to break through the outer layer that surrounds it. As soon as one sperm breaks through, it fuses with the ovum to form a new cell. The rest of the sperm cannot now enter the ovum and will die.

Sperm breaking into egg.

The new cell starts growing

The new cell, formed when the ovum and sperm join together, divides to form two identical cells. These two divide to make four, the four divide to make eight, and so on, until a solid ball of cells is formed.

The ball of cells continues to travel down the uterine tube. When it reaches the uterus, it embeds itself in the lining. This is called implantation and usually happens seven to 10 days after fertilization. Once this has happened, the woman is pregnant.

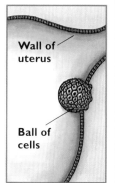

Wall of uterus

Ball of cells

Ball of cells

5

When can a woman become pregnant?

For a woman to become pregnant, a live sperm must meet one of her egg cells while it is moving along one of her uterine tubes. She usually produces one ripened egg cell each month. This is normally released about two weeks before the start of her period (see the chart). It takes a day for it to travel along the tube from her ovary to her uterus.

Sperm can survive inside a woman's uterus for about five days. There are therefore about six "fertile" days each month (five days before the egg is released and one after), when a woman may become pregnant if she has sexual intercourse without using any form of contraception (way of preventing pregnancy).

Avoiding sexual intercourse during the fertile days each month is not a reliable way to avoid getting pregnant. This is mainly because it is difficult to know exactly when ovulation is going to happen. Even women who have a regular, 28-day period cycle do not always ovulate at the expected time. It is possible for a baby to be conceived at any point during the period cycle.

Ovulating once a month. → **No longer ovulating.**

Puberty   **Menopause**   **Old age**

Continuously producing sperm. →

Puberty   **Old age**

The age when children start to develop adult bodies is called puberty. Girls usually start ovulating any time from around 11 onward. Boys usually start producing sperm from around 13 onward.

Once a boy has started producing sperm, he goes on producing them continuously, not just once a month, throughout his life. Women usually stop ovulating at around 50. This time is known as the menopause or "change of life".

An average period lasts four or five days.

Sperm entering the uterus during this time will have a chance of fertilizing the egg. This is often called the "fertile time".

Ovum released (ovulation).

Ovum travels down uterine tube.

When the ovum is released, the lining of the uterus thickens and softens, ready for the ovum to nestle in, if it is fertilized by a sperm.

If the ovum is fertilized, about seven days later it implants itself in the lining of the uterus.

If the ovum is not fertilized, the lining of the uterus starts to disintegrate.

If the ovum has implanted itself in the lining of the uterus, the woman is pregnant and does not have a period.

If the ovum has not been fertilized, two weeks after its release the lining of the uterus, mixed with blood, passes out of the woman's body as a period.

Period

1
2
3
4
5
6
7
8
9
10
11
12
13
14
15
16
17
18
19
20
21
22
23
24
25
26
27
28
29
30
31
32
33
34

period

week 1
week 2
week 3
week 4
week 5

First signs that a baby is developing

Once a fertilized egg has implanted itself in a woman's uterus, changes start to take place in her body, from which she can tell that she may be pregnant. These are some early signs:

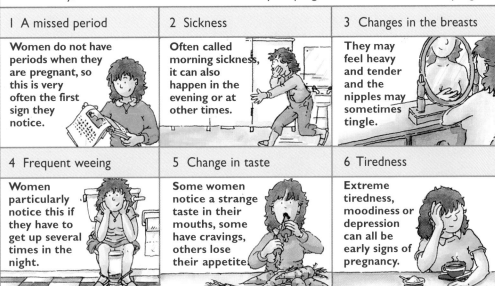

1 A missed period	2 Sickness	3 Changes in the breasts
Women do not have periods when they are pregnant, so this is very often the first sign they notice.	**Often called morning sickness, it can also happen in the evening or at other times.**	**They may feel heavy and tender and the nipples may sometimes tingle.**
4 Frequent weeing	5 Change in taste	6 Tiredness
Women particularly notice this if they have to get up several times in the night.	**Some women notice a strange taste in their mouths, some have cravings, others lose their appetite.**	**Extreme tiredness, moodiness or depression can all be early signs of pregnancy.**

You can find out why these changes occur on pages 12 and 13. To confirm that she is pregnant, a woman needs to have a pregnancy test.

Pregnancy tests

One of the main ways of confirming that a woman is pregnant is to test a sample of her urine with chemicals. The chemicals can detect certain substances which the body produces only in pregnancy.

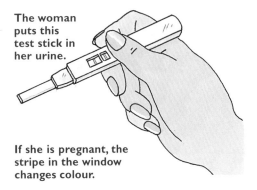

The woman puts this test stick in her urine.

If she is pregnant, the stripe in the window changes colour.

The woman can do the test herself with a kit from the chemist's, or the pharmacist, her doctor or a family planning clinic can do it for her. Some tests work as early as the first day of a missed period, although a second test may be done later to make quite sure.

Planning the pregnancy

A pregnant woman discusses with her doctor or midwife the type of care she will have during her pregnancy and where the baby will be born. A midwife is a specialist in pregnancy and birth.

Phantom pregnancy

In some very rare cases, a woman can become absolutely convinced that she is pregnant even when she is not. She shows clear signs of pregnancy, including missed periods and putting on weight. This is known as a phantom pregnancy.

7

How a baby grows inside its mother

A baby grows very rapidly inside its mother. In the first 10 weeks after its conception, it develops from a single cell into something that is recognizable as a human being. By the time it is ready to be born, it will have approximately 200 million cells. During the first 10 weeks, the developing baby is referred to as an embryo. After that it is called a fetus.

When will the baby be born?

Most babies stay inside their mothers for about 38 weeks before they are born. But because the exact date when the egg and sperm met is not usually known, the pregnancy is dated from the first day of the mother's last period, which makes it 40 weeks (10 months) long. This is roughly equal to nine calendar months (January, February etc.,) plus one extra week. Doctors and midwives usually use a chart or disc to help them work out the "expected delivery date".

January / OCTOBER
1 2 3 4 5 6 7 8 9 10 11 12 13 14 15 16 17
8 9 10 11 12 13 14 15 16 17

February / NOVEMBER
1 2 3 4 5 6 7 8 9 10
8 9 10 11 12 13 14 15 16 17

March / DECEMBER
1 2 3 4 5 6 7 8 9 10
8 9 10 11 12 13 14 15

April / JANUARY
4 5 6 7 8 9 1
9 10 11 12 13 14 1

May / FEBRUARY
5 6 7 8 9 1
9 10 11 12 13

First day of last period

Expected delivery date

The first three months

0 weeks	1 week	2 weeks	3 weeks	4 weeks	5 weeks
First day of last period		Egg is fertilized.	Egg implants in lining of uterus.	Missed period	Embryo just big enough to be visible.

6 weeks

7 weeks

At six weeks, the beginnings of a backbone and brain are forming. The heart starts to beat.

At seven weeks, four tiny swellings have developed. These are the beginnings of hands and feet.

At eight weeks, the embryo has eyes but no eyelids. It starts making its first tiny movements but its mother cannot feel them yet.

8 weeks

By 12 weeks, the baby is easily recognizable as a human being, although its head is still very large in proportion to the rest of its body. Girls and boys start to look distinctly different from each other at about this stage.

12 weeks

The baby's life support system

The human body needs food and oxygen in order to stay alive and grow. It also has to get rid of waste products. While a baby is inside its mother, it does not eat or breathe, but gets its food and oxygen from its mother's blood. Waste products are transferred from its blood to its mother's. This exchange of substances between the mother's blood and the baby's happens via a special organ called a placenta.

When the embryo first sticks to the lining of the uterus, it dissolves some of the cells beneath it, sinks inward and starts to feed off its mother's blood. It gradually grows a network of blood vessels. This mixes with a network of blood vessels grown by its mother. The two networks mixed together form the placenta. It is fully developed by the time the embryo is about 10 weeks old.

The baby is attached to the placenta by a cord leading out of its navel. This is called an umbilical cord. Blood, carrying food and oxygen, travels from the placenta through the cord to the baby's body. It travels around the baby's body and back to the placenta. On its way back it carries waste products from the baby's body. From the placenta they pass into the mother's blood.

The blood vessels of the mother and baby do not actually join each other but have a thin layer of cells separating them. This acts as a barrier and helps to prevent some, but not all, harmful substances getting through to the baby.

Placenta

Fluid

Umbilical cord

Amniotic sac

Inside the uterus, the baby becomes surrounded by a bag called the amniotic sac, caul or membranes. This bag is filled with a watery liquid (the "waters"), which acts as a shock absorber if the mother receives a bump. It also helps her to keep the baby at an even temperature and allows it to grow and move around freely.

9

16 weeks (4 months)*

The uterus is now entirely filled by the baby, placenta and waters, and gradually stretches from now on as the baby continues to grow. The baby begins to swallow and to pass urine. It has finger and toenails. At this stage its skin is bright red and transparent.

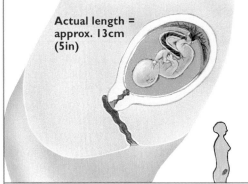

Actual length = approx. 13cm (5in)

The mother's bulge is just beginning to show and her clothes are getting tight. Any sickness she was feeling earlier has usually gone by this time.

20 weeks (5 months)

The baby's hair is starting to appear and it now has eyebrows and eyelashes. Its eyes are still tightly closed and the whole surface of its body is covered with a fine, downy hair called lanugo. Its skin is now less transparent but very wrinkled.

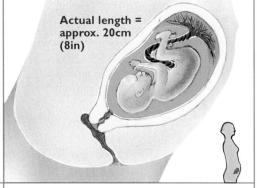

Actual length = approx. 20cm (8in)

Sometime between about 18 and 22 weeks, the mother usually begins to feel her baby moving when it wriggles about and exercises its arms and legs.

24 weeks (6 months)

The baby now has distinct periods of sleep and wakefulness. It can probably hear voices, music and other sounds from outside its mother, above the noise of her heartbeat and blood circulating. If the baby were born now, it would have a chance of surviving, provided it received expert care in a special premature baby unit.

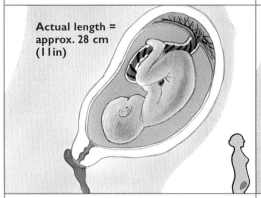

Actual length = approx. 28 cm (11in)

The mother is obviously pregnant now. The baby's heart can be heard beating through a special listening device called a fetal stethoscope.

28 weeks (7 months)

If the baby were born at this stage, it would have a good chance of surviving, but it would have to be put in an incubator because its lungs are still not well enough developed for it to breathe on its own. The baby is now covered with a thick, white grease called vernix, which helps to prevent its skin becoming waterlogged.

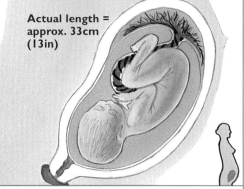

Actual length = approx. 33cm (13in)

The baby's kicks are fairly strong by now and can be felt by putting a hand on the mother's tummy. Sometimes she can feel her baby having hiccups.

*Dated from the first day of the mother's last period.

32 weeks (8 months)

The baby starts to put on some fat and become less wrinkled. Its lungs are starting to mature and get ready to take their first breath. It may begin to try sucking - some babies suck their thumbs before they are born.

36 weeks (9 months)

By now the baby has usually taken up its final position in the uterus - usually head down. From now on, it has no room to somersault around because it fills the uterus, which cannot expand any more. It continues to get fatter.

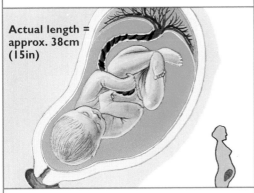

Actual length = approx. 38cm (15in)

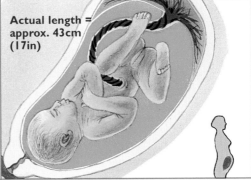

Actual length = approx. 43cm (17in)

The mother may lean back noticeably by now to counteract the baby's weight and she may walk with her legs slightly apart to help her balance.

You may be able to see the mother's tummy moving when the baby moves its limbs. Often you can guess whether the bump is a hand or a foot.

40 weeks (10 months)

Some time from 36 weeks onward, the baby's head drops down into its mother's pelvis, or "engages", ready for the birth.

Actual length = approx. 50cm (20in)

Pelvis

When the baby's head engages, the mother may be able to breathe more easily, as her lungs have been getting squashed and this allows them a little more room.

The time when the baby is fully ready to be born is referred to as "full term" or "term". 40 weeks is only an average length of pregnancy and it is perfectly normal for a baby to arrive any time between the 38th and 42nd week.

By this time the lanugo has usually disappeared, except perhaps from the shoulders, but the baby's body may still be covered with vernix.

Changes in the mother's body

When a woman is pregnant, her body undergoes a whole range of changes, adapting itself to the needs of the growing baby and preparing itself for the birth. These changes are triggered by special chemicals called hormones, which travel around her body in her blood.

The main hormones of pregnancy are progesterone and oestrogen. These are present in all women's bodies, but in pregnancy they are produced in much greater quantities than usual. They are normally produced by the ovaries, but after the first three months of pregnancy the placenta takes over this job.

The uterus

One of the most obvious changes during pregnancy is that the mother's uterus gets much bigger to make room for the growing baby inside it. The uterus is made of a type of muscle called smooth muscle. The hormone, progesterone, has the effect of relaxing smooth muscle and making it more stretchy so that it can expand more easily. Here you can see the size of the uterus at different stages of pregnancy.

The breasts

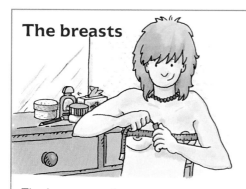

The hormones of pregnancy start preparing the breasts to produce milk and they increase considerably in size. They start making a substance called colostrum but do not produce any milk until about two or three days after the baby is born (see pages 34-35).

The pelvis

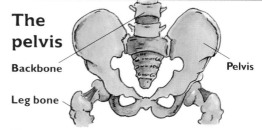

Backbone   Pelvis

Leg bone

The pelvis is the circle of bone which connects the leg bones to the bottom of the spine. It is actually made of three bones joined together by tough fibres called ligaments. When a baby is born, it has to pass through the bottom of this circle. During pregnancy, progesterone makes the ligaments softer and more stretchy, so that the pelvis can expand and let the baby through more easily.

Some inconvenient side effects

Many women feel perfectly fit and healthy throughout pregnancy, but most experience at least one or two of the complaints listed here. They are mainly caused by the increase in the amount of hormones circulating in the woman's body and the increased size of the uterus, which puts pressure on other organs and extra weight at the front of the body.

Backache
Bad balance
Breathlessness
Clumsiness

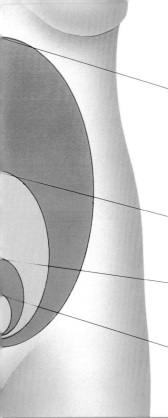

At 36 weeks - it reaches up as far as the breast bone (where the ribs join together at the front of the chest).

At 22 weeks - it reaches about the size of a football.

At 12 weeks - about the size of a grapefruit.

Before pregnancy - about the size of a small pear.

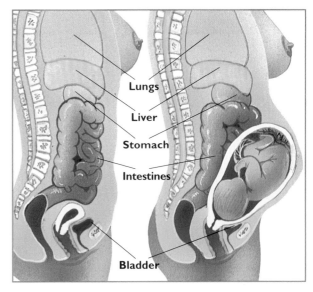

Lungs
Liver
Stomach
Intestines
Bladder

These two pictures show how the growth of the baby and the uterus squashes all the other things that normally fill the space inside the body.

The skin

Pregnant women sometimes feel noticeably warmer than usual, due to the increase in the amount of blood passing through the blood vessels in their skin. Most pregnant women also find that their moles and freckles, and the area around their nipples, become darker brown, and a dark line, the "linea nigra", appears down the middle of their abdomen.* Occasionally, dark patches also appear on the face.

The blood

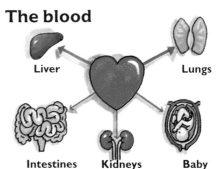

Liver
Lungs
Intestines   Kidneys   Baby

During pregnancy, the amount of blood in the mother's body can increase by as much as half, and her heart has to beat harder to pump the extra blood around her body. The extra blood helps to supply the needs of the baby and the mother's other organs, which all have to work harder than usual.

Constipation
Cramp
Emotional changes ("highs", "lows" or rapid mood changes)
Faintness
Forgetfulness
Frequent weeing
Headaches

Heartburn (burning sensation in chest)
Itchy skin
Sleeplessness
Stretch marks (pink or blue lines on skin)
Swollen ankles, feet and hands
Varicose (swollen) veins in legs
Vivid dreams
Vomiting

*The abdomen is the part of the body between the chest and the top of the legs.

Making sure the mother and baby are healthy

Pregnancy is a natural process of the body. Many women feel perfectly fit and healthy throughout and can continue doing almost all the things they usually do. However, their bodies are under a lot of extra strain and it is important that they take good care of themselves. The health of a mother and her baby are very closely linked during pregnancy.

Everyday activities

As the mother's body gets larger and the weight of the baby increases, there is a danger that the muscles in her abdomen may get overstretched. If they do, they cannot do their job properly and this may lead to backache. The loosening of the joints in the mother's body, brought about by hormones, also increases the likelihood of back problems. Whether sitting, standing, walking or lifting things, she should keep her back as straight as possible. She needs to be especially careful when doing any of the activities shown on the right.

Lifting and carrying heavy weights: might cause back strain.

Leaning forward: might cause back strain.

Standing still for a long time: bad for blood circulation.

Balancing: balance not good, might fall.

Exercise, rest and relaxation

It is sensible for pregnant women to keep up any exercise they are used to. Special exercises to strengthen muscles and prepare the body to give birth can be helpful, as can exercises which help the body to relax. A tense body cannot rest properly and during pregnancy it is important to get plenty of rest.

Going to classes

Classes offer people a chance to meet others in the same situation, discuss feelings, exchange information and learn about pregnancy, birth and becoming parents. They can also try out relaxation techniques and positions to help the mother during pregnancy and while giving birth.

Putting on weight

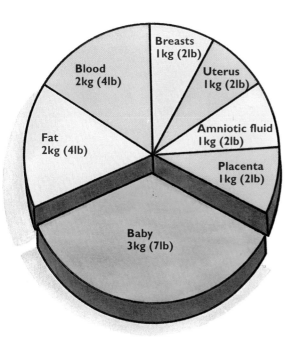

Breasts
1kg (2lb)

Uterus
1kg (2lb)

Blood
2kg (4lb)

Amniotic fluid
1kg (2lb)

Fat
2kg (4lb)

Placenta
1kg (2lb)

Baby
3kg (7lb)

Most women gain between 9kg (approx. 20lbs) and 13kg (approx. 28lbs) while they are pregnant. The extra weight gain is made up roughly as shown in the chart above. As you can see, only a fairly small proportion of the extra weight is fat.

Eating well

While a woman is pregnant, it is even more important than usual that she eats a healthy diet consisting of a wide variety of good, fresh food. The food she eats supplies her baby's needs as well as her own and the baby will take what it needs, even if this does not leave enough to keep the mother healthy. She will probably want to eat a little more than usual but may find that she can only eat small amounts at a time, especially toward the end of pregnancy, because her stomach is squashed into a smaller space.

Things that can hurt an unborn baby

Just as food and oxygen can pass through the placenta to the unborn baby, so can other things which the mother takes into her body. Some of these can damage the baby, especially during the first three months of its existence, when its body is developing very rapidly. At this stage the parents often do not yet know that the baby is there. This is one reason why it is important for parents to plan pregnancies.

Many medicines and other drugs can pass through the placenta and some can be harmful. A pregnant woman should check with her doctor or midwife before she takes any medicines, even those she can buy without a prescription.

 Babies of mothers who smoke tend to be underweight and have feeding problems, and are more at risk of catching certain infections when they are first born. There is also evidence to suggest that babies of fathers who smoke are more likely to experience these problems.

Alcohol crosses the placenta and should be avoided altogether in pregnancy or taken only in small amounts.

A few infectious diseases can damage a baby if its mother has them early in pregnancy. The most common one is German measles (rubella) which can affect a baby's heart, sight or hearing. Many girls and women are now immunized against rubella, but this must not be done during or immediately before a pregnancy.

Medical checkups

Pregnant women need to have regular checkups to make sure that the baby is growing and developing normally, and to check that the mother is not developing any problems that might seriously affect her or the baby. The checkups may take place at a hospital, health centre, doctor's surgery, midwife's clinic or in the mother's home. They are called antenatal ("before birth") checkups. Doctors specializing in pregnancy are called obstetricians. A midwife is a specialist in pregnancy but is not a doctor.

1  On her first visit to the clinic, a sample of blood is taken and tested to check general health and detect any problems that might affect the baby. More blood tests are taken later in pregnancy.

2  A sample of the mother's urine is tested with chemicals at every visit. The presence of certain substances, such as sugar or protein, can give warning that problems are developing in her body.

3  The mother's weight is checked regularly. After the first three months she should gain weight slowly but steadily. This is good for the growing baby and for breast-feeding.

4  At every visit her blood pressure (the force with which the heart pumps blood around the body) is measured. High blood pressure can affect the baby's growth and cause problems for the mother.

5  The midwife or doctor examines the mother's uterus by feeling it through her abdomen. Its size gives a good indication of how well the baby is growing. Later in pregnancy, they can feel the baby's position.

6  The baby's heartbeat is checked through a listening device called a fetal stethoscope. A special machine may be used which electronically amplifies the sound of the baby's heart.

Ultrasound examination

This is a method of examining an unborn baby by sending sound waves, far above the range of human hearing, into the mother's body. The waves bounce back off the surfaces they meet inside the body and these echoes are measured and translated into dots of light. The dots are used to build up a picture of the baby on a screen similar to a TV screen.

This method can be used to assess the age, size and growth rate of a baby. It will also show whether the mother is going to have twins, long before she or her doctor would normally suspect they are there.

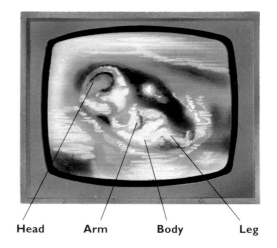

Head   **Arm**   **Body**   **Leg**

Testing for abnormalities

Most babies are born perfectly healthy, but a small percentage have a physical or mental disability. There are a number of tests that can be done during pregnancy to see whether a baby has any problems. Blood tests and ultrasound examinations may indicate certain abnormalities. If they do, or there is a possibility that the baby may have inherited some abnormality, doctors may suggest doing one of the tests shown below. These tests are done with great care not to damage the baby.

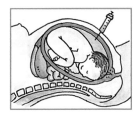

I The fluid in the amniotic sac surrounding the baby contains some of the baby's cells. Some of this fluid can be obtained by a method called amniocentesis. First the mother has an injection of local anaesthetic to numb a small patch of skin on her abdomen. Then a hollow needle is passed through her skin into her uterus. A small sample of fluid is sucked out into a syringe attached to the end of the needle and sent to a laboratory for tests.

2 One instrument designed to check the health of an unborn baby is called a fetoscope. It is a very small telescope mounted on the end of a hollow needle. When the needle is passed through the mother's abdomen and into her uterus, the doctor can look through it and see the baby. It is even possible to take photographs through a fetoscope.

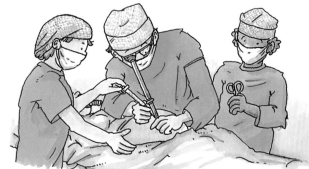

Finding out what sex the baby will be

There are many myths about how to tell what sex a baby will be, but at present the only reliable method of prediction involves examining one of the baby's cells. If, for particular medical reasons, the mother has an amniocentesis, the doctors can tell whether she will have a boy or a girl. However, in many cases the parents ask not to be told.

What is a miscarriage?

A baby born at the 24th week of pregnancy stands a chance of surviving. A baby born earlier than this usually dies. This is known as a miscarriage. There are many reasons why miscarriages may happen and often the cause is not known. They are unfortunately very common, especially in the early stages of pregnancy. It is thought that many early miscarriages happen because the baby is not developing normally. A miscarriage is sometimes referred to as a "spontaneous abortion".

What is an abortion?

If the doctors have reason to believe that a baby is likely to be seriously mentally or physically disabled, or that the mother could be badly damaged physically or mentally by continuing with a pregnancy, the parents sometimes decide that it would be better if the baby did not survive. If they do, the mother goes into a hospital or clinic and the baby is removed from her uterus. This is called an abortion or "termination of pregnancy".

How a baby is born

The process by which a baby leaves its mother's uterus and emerges into the world is called labour or childbirth. It happens in three stages. Nobody knows exactly what causes labour to start. Most evidence suggests that when a baby has reached the point where it is ready to be born, it produces hormones which reach its mother's body through the placenta and trigger it into labour.

The length of time that labour lasts varies immensely. The average time for a first baby is about 12-15 hours, but it can be much longer or much shorter than this. The time tends to get shorter with each baby a woman has.

First stage

During the first stage of labour, the bottom part of the uterus opens up enough to give the baby room to get out. This part of the uterus, which separates it from the vagina, is called the cervix. In the middle of the cervix there is a tiny opening or passage, which is normally only about 2mm wide.

At the end of pregnancy, the uterus is the largest and one of the most powerful muscles in the body. During labour the muscle in the upper part of the uterus keeps contracting (becoming smaller) and then relaxing again. The contractions gradually pull the cervix open. After each contraction the uterus remains slightly smaller than it was before, so the baby's head becomes firmly pressed against the cervix, helping it to open up.

The average diameter of a newborn baby's head is 9.5cm (approx. 4in), so the opening in the cervix has to reach about 10cm to allow it to go through. At some point the pressure on the bag of waters surrounding the baby becomes so great that the bag breaks. The fluid runs out through the cervix and vagina.

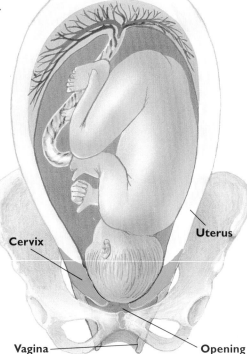

Cervix
Uterus
Vagina
Opening

Contractions

The first stage is the longest part of labour. The average length for a first baby is about 10 hours. In early labour the contractions may be 20 or 30 minutes apart, but as the labour progresses they gradually get more frequent and stronger. By the time the cervix is fully opened, the uterus will be contracting about every two minutes and the contractions lasting about one and a half minutes.

Pattern of first stage contractions

Second stage

The second stage of labour starts when the cervix is fully open and ends with the baby actually being born or "delivered". This stage may take anything from a few minutes to about two hours.

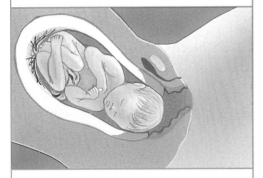

Between leaving the uterus and emerging from its mother's body, the baby travels through the vagina or "birth canal". The walls of the vagina have folds or pleats in them, so when the baby passes through they can expand to make room.

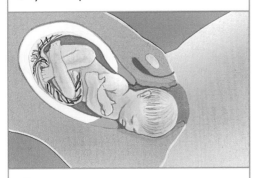

The uterus continues to contract at regular intervals and during the contractions the mother feels an urge to use her muscles to push the baby out. Once the baby's head has passed out of the vagina, the rest of its body usually slips out fairly easily.

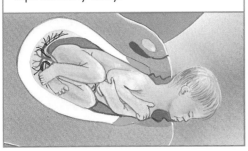

Third stage

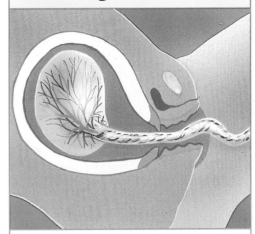

When the baby is born, it is still attached to the placenta by its umbilical cord, and the placenta is still attached to the wall of the uterus. Shortly after the birth, the placenta detaches itself from the uterus and passes through the vagina and out of the mother's body. The empty amniotic sac, which is still attached to the placenta, comes with it. The placenta, the sac and the cord are sometimes called the "afterbirth".

How does the mother know labour is starting?

For the mother, the first sign that labour is starting may be when she becomes aware of cramp-like pains coming at regular intervals, perhaps 20 or 30 minutes apart. They are caused by the contractions of her uterus and are usually felt low down in the abdomen or at the bottom of the back. She may also notice the whole of her abdomen tightening during the contractions.

Sometimes the bag of waters bursts before she notices any contractions, and she feels fluid running out of her vagina.

When she goes to the toilet, she may notice that a small lump of mucus has passed out of her body. (This is known as a "show".) It has acted as a plug in the middle of her cervix throughout pregnancy, but when the cervix starts to open, it drops out.

Checking the progress of labour

Whether a baby is born in hospital or at home, the mother is usually looked after by a midwife during labour. The midwife helps and encourages her and does regular checks to make sure everything is going well.

The midwife can check how the labour is progressing by feeling with her fingers inside the vagina how far the cervix has opened. When it reaches nearly 10cm (4in), she knows that the first stage is coming to an end. She may also want to check the mother's pulse, temperature and blood pressure from time to time.

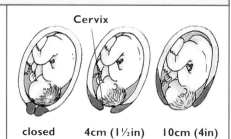

Cervix

closed   4cm (1½in)   10cm (4in)

By feeling the mother's abdomen, the midwife can check the timing and strength of the contractions and by listening to the baby's heartbeat, she can tell how the baby is. Occasionally the baby can get short of oxygen, which could be dangerous.

Hospitals have machines called monitors, which can be used to record the baby's heartbeat. The monitor shown in this picture is a portable one. When the transducer is held on the mother's abdomen, the baby's heartbeat is heard through the loudspeaker of the audio unit. Some larger, non-portable monitors record the contractions as well as the heartbeat.

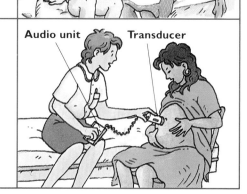

Audio unit   Transducer

What happens when the baby is born?

Most babies are born head first. When the chest is born, the baby can expand its lungs and start to breathe. Once the rest of the body has emerged, the midwife or doctor checks that its mouth and nose are clear of liquid.

At this stage, the baby is still attached to the placenta by its umbilical cord and the placenta is still inside the mother. After a few minutes, the cord is clamped in two places and then cut between the clamps.

The mother and father can then hold and cuddle their baby and take a good look at it. Some babies cry a lot soon after they are born, some very little or not at all. Crying can help them to fill their lungs with air and clear them of fluid.

Helping the mother

Having a baby is a very exciting experience but it can also be painful and exhausting. Contractions are also known as "labour pains". Although they usually start as a fairly mild aching sensation, they become more painful as they get more frequent and stronger throughout the first stage. The end of the first stage is generally the most painful time of the whole labour. The second stage is very hard work for the mother and by the time the baby is born, she is often quite exhausted. Many fathers now share the experience with the mother and see their babies born. They can give a great deal of help and encouragement. There are several things that can be done to make the experience less painful.

1 Pain feels much worse when you are tense. If the mother can breathe steadily and evenly during contractions and relax her body between them, it helps to reduce her tension and pain. Massage may help her to relax.

2 If she wants, she can have an injection of a pain-relieving drug. As well as relieving her pain, the drug may make her drowsy. It can also cross the placenta and may make the baby a little drowsy when it is born.

3 She can choose to have some "gas and air". This is a mixture of nitrous oxide (laughing gas) and oxygen, which she breathes in through a mask every time she gets a contraction.

4 She can have an "epidural block". This is an injection of local anaesthetic into her back, which numbs the nerves around her spine and takes away all feeling from the lower half of her body.

After being checked to see that everything is normal, the baby is weighed and its length and head size are measured. It is important to know its birth weight as, from now on, regular weight checks are the best way of telling that it is growing well.

It is very important to keep the baby warm. Babies can lose heat rapidly, especially from their wet heads. After being cuddled by their parents, weighed and perhaps given a bath, they must be wrapped up warm.

If a baby is born in hospital, it has a label attached to its wrist, giving its name and the date and time it was born. The mother may have a matching label attached to her wrist. This avoids any confusion about who the baby belongs to.

Helping to start labour

Sometimes the medical staff looking after a pregnant woman may think it advisable to start her labour off artificially rather than waiting for it to happen naturally. This is called "inducing" labour. They usually do this by giving her hormones, either in a special tablet (pessary) which dissolves when placed in her vagina, or in a fluid dripped into a vein in her arm via a needle (this method is usually referred to as "a drip").

Using forceps to help with the birth

Sometimes the doctor needs to use forceps to speed up the second stage of labour. If this stage goes on too long, the baby may get short of oxygen. The ends of the forceps fit closely around the baby's head and the doctor gently pulls the baby out. Instead of using forceps, a doctor may use a suction device called a vacuum extractor or Ventouse.*

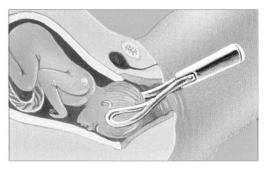

Cutting and stitching

Sometimes the skin and muscle around the entrance to the vagina tears, when it stretches to let the baby's head through. A cut may be made to prevent this happening. If forceps are used or the baby is in the breech position (see next page), a cut is nearly always made. After the birth, tears and cuts are repaired with stitches. They can be fairly sore for several days after the birth.

Babies who need special care

Some babies are born needing special care. There are a number of reasons why this may be necessary. The baby may be premature (born more than three weeks before the expected date), or particularly small and light, or it may have some infection or defect. A baby like this is usually put in an incubator (an enclosed, transparent cot) and given special attention by doctors and nurses. Most babies who need special medical care during the first few days or weeks of their lives, grow into normal, healthy babies.

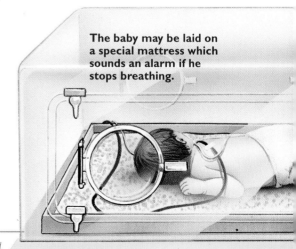

The baby may be laid on a special mattress which sounds an alarm if he stops breathing.

*Suction is applied via a metal cup placed on the baby's head.

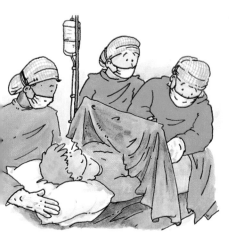

What is a Caesarian birth?

A Caesarian is a method of delivering a baby by cutting through the mother's abdomen and uterus and lifting the baby and placenta out. The complete operation takes about 40 minutes. The mother may have a general anaesthetic so that she is asleep during it, but it is fairly common to have an epidural block (see page 21) instead. This numbs the lower half of the mother's body so she can stay awake to see her baby born without feeling any pain.

A Caesarian is necessary if the baby cannot get out of the uterus because its mother's pelvis is too small or the placenta is blocking its path. It is also needed if the health of the mother or baby is at risk unless the baby is born quickly.

What is a breech birth?

Most babies are born head first but a few do not turn into this position before labour starts and are born bottom or "breech" first. The birth is a little more difficult if the baby is in this position.

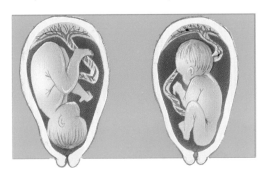

Natural childbirth

Giving birth is a natural process for a woman's body but it does carry some risks for both mothers and babies. In an attempt to make childbirth safer there has been a move toward delivering most babies in hospital. Over the last 30 years, there have also been developments in technology, so that labour can now be artificially started, speeded up, made less painful and more easily monitored.

There are disadvantages to the use of too much technology, however, and many people, including doctors and midwives, feel that it is better only to intervene in the natural course of events in labour for very specific medical reasons. They feel that the more a woman and her partner know about what happens in labour, how to help its progress and what medical help is available, the more satisfying and rewarding the experience will be. This attitude toward labour is sometimes referred to as the "natural childbirth movement".

The temperature inside the incubator is carefully controlled. The baby does not need to wear anything except a nappy and can be observed more easily without clothes.

He may be fed by passing a tube through his nose and down into his stomach, or through a drip into a vein.

He can quickly be given extra oxygen if necessary.

What is a stillbirth?

A stillbirth is the birth of a dead baby after more than 24 weeks of pregnancy.* This is always a very sad event for the baby's parents and family but, in Western countries, it is now much less common than it used to be. This is due to improvements in the medical care of pregnant women and the early detection of possible problems affecting either the baby or the mother.

*Before this, it is a miscarriage or abortion (see page 17).

What makes a baby like it is?

From the instant of conception, when an ovum and a sperm join together inside the mother's body to form one new cell, that cell already contains all the information needed to construct a new and unique human being. The instructions inside each cell that tell the body how to develop are called genes. The way a person develops does not depend on genes alone. The people and things that surround them, their food and climate all influence their development as well.

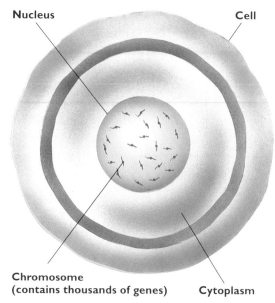

Nucleus

Cell

Chromosome (contains thousands of genes)

Cytoplasm

1 The human body starts as just one cell which, by dividing again and again, very quickly develops into billions of cells. Most of the cells in the body are so tiny that they can only be seen through a microscope. Each cell consists of a jelly-like substance called cytoplasm, with a nucleus in the middle. The nucleus contains thread-like structures called chromosomes. Each chromosome is made up of thousands of genes.

2 Genes are like an incredibly complicated computer, which can store and classify very detailed information. Each gene is made up of chemicals joined together to look similar to a twisted ladder. The order of the chemicals in the rungs of the ladder varies and forms a code. A sequence of about 250 rungs gives the instructions for one particular characteristic such as hair colour.

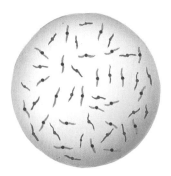

One of each pair of chromosomes comes from the mother and one from the father.

3 Each ovum and each sperm contains 23 chromosomes. When the two join together, the new cell therefore has 46 chromosomes (23 pairs). An exact copy of these 46 chromosomes is passed to every cell in the baby's body and stays with it for life.

Boy or girl?

Out of the 23 chromosomes in each ovum and each sperm, one is a sex chromosome. There are two types of sex chromosomes. They are called "X" and "Y". All ova have an X chromosome. Half a man's sperm have an X chromosome, the other half have a Y. If a sperm with an X chromosome joins the ovum, the baby will be a girl. If a sperm with a Y chromosome joins the ovum, the baby will be a boy.

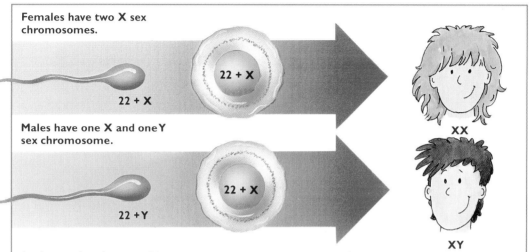

Females have two **X** sex chromosomes.

22 + X

22 + X

XX

Males have one **X** and one **Y** sex chromosome.

22 + X

22 + Y

XY

In theory, the chances of having a boy or a girl should be exactly equal. Nobody really knows why some parents seem to produce only boys and others only girls. It is thought that male sperm swim faster but female sperm live longer. Therefore, if a couple have intercourse at the same time as, or after, ovulation, there is more chance of conceiving a boy; if before ovulation, there is more chance of conceiving a girl.

Which parent will the baby look like?

Many thousands of genes from both parents influence a child's appearance, but instructions about a few characteristics, such as colour of hair and eyes, are carried by just one gene from each parent. If the instructions in these two genes conflict, one of them will overrule the other. This one is said to be the "dominant" gene, while the weaker one is said to be "recessive". The genes of the parents shown here could be combined to produce three different hair colours in their children. A dark hair gene overrules other hair colours. A fair hair gene is dominant over a red hair gene. To have red hair, you have to inherit a red hair gene from both your parents.

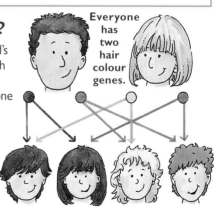

Everyone has two hair colour genes.

Dark + fair   Dark + red   Fair + red   Red + red

Abnormal genes

Sometimes a baby acquires an extra chromosome from one or both parents. Down's syndrome babies have three of a certain type of chromosome instead of the usual pair, so the baby has 47 chromosomes altogether instead of 46. This affects the baby's physical and mental development.

Some other disorders which are caused by abnormal genes are passed down from one generation to the next. If there is a family history of a particular disorder, a doctor who specializes in the study of genes can advise a couple on the chances of having a baby affected by it.

Twins, triplets and test tube babies

The chances of a mother producing twins are about one in 80. In some races they are more common and in some less common than this. A family history of twins, on either the mother's or the father's side, makes twins more likely. Twins, triplets etc. are often referred to as "multiple births".

How do twins start?

There are two types of twins - identical and non-identical (fraternal). Identical twins start when a fertilized egg splits in half at a very early stage in its development. Each half develops into a baby.* The twins have identical genes, are the same sex and exactly alike.

Non-identical twins start when two eggs are released from the mother's ovaries at the same time and are joined by two sperm. These twins may be no more alike than any brother and sister. They may be the same sex or one of each and do not have identical genes.

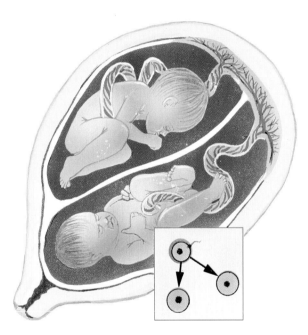

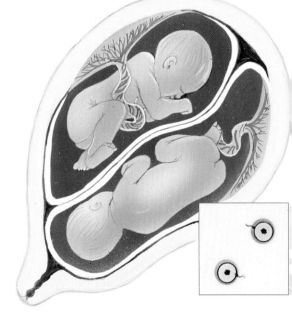

Identical twins share a placenta. The fluid surrounding them is separated by a thin layer of cells enclosed in a common outer layer.

Non-identical twins each have their own placenta and each is surrounded by its own bag of fluid.

Diagnosing twins

Sometimes a midwife or doctor may suspect that a woman is going to have twins because her abdomen is much larger than it should be. Sometimes they can detect two heartbeats or feel two heads or lots of limbs. If the mother has an ultrasound scan (see page 16), the twins can usually be detected by the 14th week of pregnancy.

How twins are born

Labour for a mother giving birth to twins is very similar to labour for a woman having only one baby. It does not usually take longer. There is only one first stage, because once the uterus has opened up, both babies can get out. The second stage is usually very quick for the second baby, because the birth canal has already been stretched by the first.

26

*If an egg starts to divide but does not completely separate, Siamese twins are produced. This is very rare.

Triplets and more

The chance of having triplets is about one in 6,400. Having more than three babies at a time used to be extremely rare. These days, the use of special drugs designed to help women who could not have babies, can sometimes have the effect of stimulating their ovaries to produce more than one egg at a time. Three or more babies can be either identical or non-identical, or a combination of both.

Identical (all from one egg)

Non-identical (from three separate eggs)

Two identical, one non-identical

Problems in starting a baby

Couples may be unable to have a child or have problems in starting one for a variety of reasons. It may be that the woman is not ovulating, or that the man is not producing healthy sperm, or that the tubes which carry the ova or sperm have become blocked or damaged in some way. Sometimes doctors can give drugs to stimulate ovulation or sperm production. Sometimes they can repair the tubes.

Test tube babies

In vitro fertilization is a method of helping couples who seem unable to start a baby, especially in cases where the cause is blocked uterine tubes. *In vitro* means "in glass" and the method is so-called because test tubes are used in the process. The timing of each step in the process, and the temperature and chemical conditions in which the egg and sperm are kept, have to be extremely carefully controlled for the result to be successful.

The doctor inserts a tube through the woman's abdomen to her ovary, and the ovum she has produced that month is drawn out by suction.

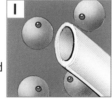
1

The ovum is put in a dish and the father's sperm is added. One of the sperm fuses with the egg, which then starts to divide and subdivide.

2

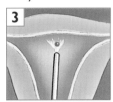
3

When it has eight or 16 cells, it is put back into the mother's uterus, via a tube inserted through her vagina and cervix.

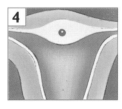
4

If the fertilized ovum implants itself in the wall of the uterus, it will start to grow there, as in any normal pregnancy.

In cases of *in vitro* fertilization, the woman is often given drugs to encourage her to produce more than one ripened ovum at a time. Several ova are then taken, fertilized and returned to the uterus, to increase the chances of at least one implanting itself. Sometimes they all do.

It is possible to freeze a fertilized ovum for implantation in the uterus at some future date. This means that if one attempt to start a pregnancy is unsuccessful, another can be made without having to operate again to remove ova. Frozen embryos can also be kept in case an attempt is unsuccessful, or a mother wants more children after a successful "test tube" pregnancy.

Newborn babies

All babies look different and individual, even when they are newly born, but here are a few things you may notice if you see a very new one.

Many babies have dark blue eyes when they are born, though they may start to change to a different colour very soon after birth. They may also appear to squint, because they cannot hold both eyes in line for very long.

Some babies are born with quite a mop of hair; others are almost bald. In the womb, babies are completely covered by fine, downy hair. Sometimes they still have some on their bodies and faces, but it soon rubs off.

For the first few days, a small piece of the umbilical cord remains attached to the baby's navel. It is tied and sealed with a clip, and soon dries out and falls off.

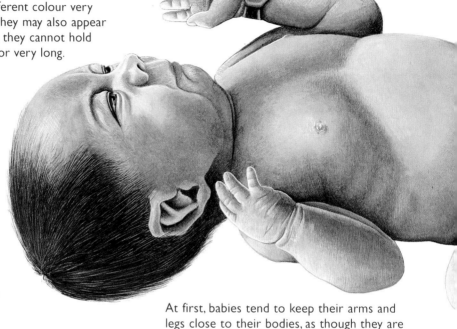

At first, babies tend to keep their arms and legs close to their bodies, as though they are still enclosed in the womb.

What is birth like for a baby?

Birth is an experience we have all been through but cannot consciously remember, so we can only imagine what it must be like.

For nine months a baby grows in warmth and comfort in her mother's uterus, surrounded by liquid, darkness and the constant rhythmic sounds of her mother's body. She does not have to breathe or eat; her needs are constantly supplied via her mother's blood.

Suddenly everything changes. The walls of the uterus close in around her, squeezing and pushing her through the narrow passageway to an outside world which is full of completely new sensations. Immediately, her whole body has to adapt to a life more independent of her mother.

She has to start breathing and, within a few hours. taking in food, digesting it and expelling her own wastes.

It must come as a great shock to even the most tranquil baby to experience so many new sensations in such a short time. Babies react to this in different ways: some are tired and sleep a great deal at first, others are wide awake; some are upset and jumpy, others serene and contented. Whatever a baby's temperament, most people agree that it is important to introduce a baby to the world as gently as possible, especially during the first few hours after birth. Dim lighting, gentle handling and peaceful surroundings can help to reassure her and make the world a less alarming place.

Many babies develop yellowish skin a few days after birth. This is because it takes a little while before their livers start working properly, so they have slight jaundice. This does not harm them and usually goes away without any treatment.

It is very common for newborn babies to have rashes, spots and marks on their skin, which may also be dry and peel a little during the first few days.

Their finger and toenails are fully formed and sometimes fairly long, but very soft.

On the top of a baby's head, near the front, there is a diamond-shaped patch under the skin, which is not covered by the skull bone. This is called the fontanelle. It usually takes a year or so before the bone completely closes over it. The fontanelle allows the skull bones to overlap a little during the birth, so that the head becomes moulded to the shape of the birth canal. This can give it a strange elongated appearance at first. After a few days it becomes rounder.

New parents

The arrival of a new baby is a very exciting time for the parents and the rest of the family. It is also a time when everyone has to adjust to the presence of a brand new person in their lives. A first child usually brings about great changes in his parents' lives. It takes time to learn how to look after a baby and to get used to being a parent. At first they can feel a bit alarmed, overwhelmed and exhausted.

Getting to know a new baby

It can take varying amounts of time for parents to get to know their new baby and really feel that he belongs to them. Sometimes this happens as soon as he is born, but sometimes he seems like a stranger at first and it takes several days or weeks for a specially close relationship to develop.

It is important that a father has time with his baby and learns to help look after him. The tie between a baby and his mother can be so close that fathers can easily feel left out and jealous.

Brothers and sisters can also feel jealous. However excited they are about the new baby, it can be very hard to see so much attention given to someone new. It helps if they too can spend time with the baby and help to look after him.

The mother's body

It takes only a few weeks for the main changes in the mother's body to reverse themselves after birth, but it is usually several months before its complete return to normal. The changes start happening the moment the placenta leaves her uterus, since it is the placenta that produces most of the hormones of pregnancy. This sudden change in hormone levels often affects the mother's emotions, making her feel a bit tearful and depressed. Occasionally the hormone balance in her body fails to readjust itself and she needs medical treatment for "post-natal" (after birth) depression.

The uterus

By about six weeks after the birth, the uterus has returned to its normal size. As it shrinks, it contracts and relaxes at irregular intervals. These contractions, known as "after pains", feel similar to period pains and are most obvious in the first few days after the birth.

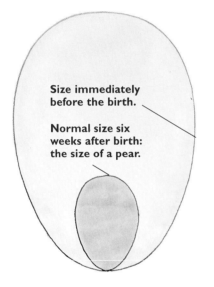

Size immediately before the birth.

Normal size six weeks after birth: the size of a pear.

As the uterus shrinks, the extra blood that supplied it is squeezed out, and its thick lining, built up during pregnancy, disintegrates. These pass out of the vagina like a period for up to five or six weeks after the birth.

A new mother needs plenty of rest after her baby is born. The birth itself, the changes taking place in her body and caring for the new baby all use up a great deal of energy.

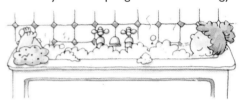

If she has had stitches to repair the skin around her vagina, walking and sitting down will be uncomfortable for a week or so. Hot baths are soothing and help her skin to heal.

Women can usually lose all the extra weight gained during pregnancy but it may take a few months to go. Exercise can help to get rid of it and strengthen muscles that have been stretched. They should also do special exercises designed to strengthen the muscles in the back, abdomen and vagina.

How soon can another baby start?

A woman does not usually start to ovulate (release eggs) and have periods for at least six weeks after the birth of a baby. From this time onward, she needs to use contraception when having sexual intercourse, unless she wants to start another baby. It may, however, be several months before she starts to ovulate again. Breast-feeding tends to delay but does not prevent it.

Helping to look after a new baby

When there is a new baby in a family, people usually appreciate all the help they can get, as it is a busy time. The best way of helping may be by doing some shopping, cleaning, washing or cooking. You may also be able to help by looking after the baby. This page gives you an idea of what small babies spend their time doing, but remember that the amount of time spent sleeping, crying or feeding will vary a great deal from one individual to another. The next two pages give some suggestions about how you might help to look after one. Never try to do anything without asking the parents exactly what they want you to do.

Most babies spend between 14 and 18 hours asleep each day, during the first three months of their lives. They sleep in short stretches and wake to feed every few hours throughout the day and night. As they get older, they begin to sleep more at night than during the day.

Crying is a baby's only way of saying that he needs something or that something is wrong, so many babies cry a lot, especially in the first few weeks. Until they are about a month old, crying is more or less the only sound that babies can make, apart from little snuffles and grunts.

Most young babies need food about every three or four hours, though some may want to feed more often than this. The only food they need is milk, which they get from sucking at a breast or bottle.* They are born knowing instinctively how to suck and swallow.

Newborn babies have very little control over their movements. They have such a strong grip that they can hang from the midwife's fingers. However, this is a reflex (automatic) action and soon disappears. It is a few months before they can grasp things on purpose.

From the moment they are born, babies start using their senses of sight, hearing, smell, touch and taste to learn about the world around them. At first they can only see things clearly if they are about 20cm (8in) from their faces. Everything else is blurred. Over the first few weeks they gradually learn to change the focus of their eyes.

*See pages 34-37.

What to do if a baby cries

The sound of a baby's crying varies according to what is wrong, but it is often difficult, even for his parents, to work out what he is trying to say. If a baby cries while you are looking after him and there is no obvious reason, try running through a list of possible causes:

1. He may be hungry - when did he last have a feed?
2. His nappy may need to be changed (see pages 38-39).
3. Wind may be making him feel uncomfortable or giving him a pain (see page 37).
4. He may be too hot or too cold. (Feel down the back of his neck.)
5. He might be bored or lonely and want some company or entertainment (see below).
6. He may be tired but unable to get to sleep (see opposite page).

Keeping a baby happy

If a baby does not appear to be hungry, tired or uncomfortable, try some of the things shown below to keep him entertained.

1. Give him things to look at. Babies like looking at bright things, things that move and, above all, people's faces.

2. Give him something to listen to. Babies usually enjoy music and rhythmic noises, and sometimes move their arms and legs in time to the sound. They also like listening to people's voices.

3. Hold him. Babies like the feeling of being held. When you pick a baby up or put him down, keep one hand under his neck and the other under his bottom. Always be careful to keep his head supported because he cannot support it himself. Hold him upright, looking over your shoulder, or lying back with his head supported by the crook of your arm.

4. Rock him. Most babies enjoy the sensation of gentle movement. Try walking up and down while holding him, rocking him in your arms or a cradle, or pushing him in a pram.

5. Sucking gives babies comfort and pleasure. Some like to suck even when they are not hungry. Some mothers give their babies dummies; others help them to find their thumb.

Helping a baby get to sleep

Some babies fall asleep easily when they are tired, others need help to get to sleep, particularly at certain times of day. Sucking, being rocked or pushed in a pram and gentle background noise may all help to relax her.

Parents are advised to put their babies to sleep on their sides or backs, not their fronts. Once a baby gets used to a certain position, she may not go to sleep in any other. She cannot turn over by herself at first.

Sometimes the jerks and twitches of her own body as it relaxes into sleep will disturb a baby. She may settle more easily if she is wrapped in a shawl. It should hold her arms firmly to her sides, but her hands should be where she can suck them if she wants to.

Getting a bath ready

It is quite difficult to hold a slippery baby safely in a bathful of water, especially if the baby does not enjoy baths. The best way to help with a bath is by getting ready everything that will be needed.

Some mothers bath their babies every day, but some simply wash their faces, hands and bottoms daily and bath them every few days. The rest of their bodies do not get very dirty until they start moving around.

An ordinary bath is too large and frightening for a tiny baby. Most people use a portable baby bath or bowl for the first few months. A portable bath usually has a stand and you can adjust its height so the bather can sit comfortably on a chair.

1. Use a bowl or jug to fill the bath with water. Always put the cold water in first. If you put the hot in first, the plastic of the bath might heat up and scald the baby.

2. Test the water with your elbow - your hands are used to hotter water than the rest of your body. It should feel comfortably warm. Make sure the room is also warm.

3. Collect everything else that will be needed. This includes:
Soap or special baby bath liquid
Cotton wool
Towel
Clean clothes
Nappy changing equipment

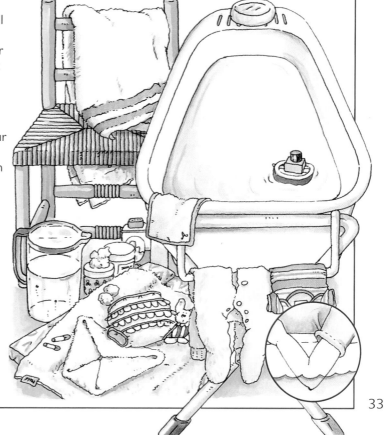

33

Feeding

For the first few months of their lives the only food that babies need is milk, either from their mothers' breasts or from bottles. After this, they gradually start to have other foods as well as milk and by the time they are about one, they are eating most ordinary foods.

Human beings are mammals, which means they produce milk to feed their young. This is the main purpose of women's breasts. Every woman's breasts contain cells for producing milk, but they do not become active unless she has a baby. The changes that prompt the breasts to start producing milk begin during pregnancy and are brought about by the special chemicals called hormones, which are produced by glands* and travel around the body in the blood. The most important hormones involved in the process of breast-feeding are produced by the pituitary gland, which lies at the base of the brain.

How breast-feeding works

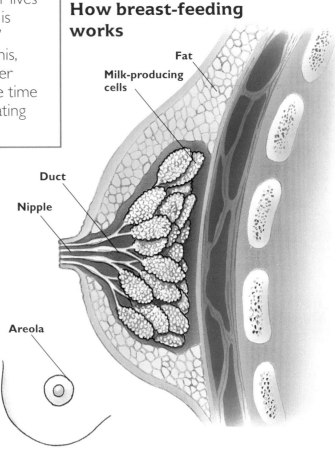

Fat

Milk-producing cells

Duct

Nipple

Areola

The area around the nipple is called the areola. The tiny bumps in the areola are glands. During breast-feeding these produce a fluid which helps to protect the nipple and keep it soft and supple.

Some advantages of breast-feeding

Breast milk contains all the ingredients a baby needs in the right proportions and at the right temperature. It is easy for babies to digest and contains germ-fighting proteins called antibodies, which help to protect them from infections. Breast-feeding can give a mother a special feeling of closeness to her baby.

Why some mothers do not breast-feed

Breast-feeding only works well if the mother is happy to be doing it, and some women dislike it or find it embarrassing. How they feel about it depends a lot on the attitudes of their husbands and their family and friends. Some are put off by initial problems, such as sore nipples. A few have medical problems that prevent them from doing it.

*To find out what a gland is, see page 47.

Each breast contains milk-producing cells and a network of tubes or ducts, which lead to an opening in the nipple. The milk-producing cells are surrounded by muscle cells and covered by layers of fat, which give each breast its individual shape and size. The fat plays no part in actually making milk, so small breasts are just as good at producing milk as large ones.

During pregnancy the number of ducts and milk-producing cells increases, replacing some of the fat, and the blood supply to the breasts increases. The birth of the baby changes the hormone levels in the blood and these signal to the breasts to start producing milk. The milk is made from substances extracted from the mother's blood as it passes through her breasts. Once made, it drains into the ducts.

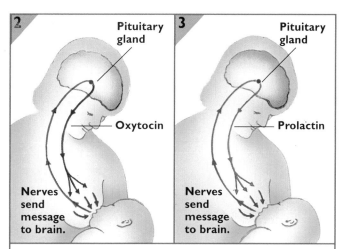

2 Pituitary gland — Oxytocin — Nerves send message to brain.

3 Pituitary gland — Prolactin — Nerves send message to brain.

A baby sucking at its mother's breast stimulates sensitive nerve-endings in the nipple, which send messages to the brain. The brain instructs the pituitary gland to produce a hormone called oxytocin. Oxytocin makes the muscle cells around the milk-producing cells and ducts contract and this forces milk down the ducts and out of the nipples. This process is known as the "let-down reflex". It only works if the mother is feeling relaxed and calm.

The baby's sucking also stimulates the pituitary gland to produce another important hormone, called prolactin. This is the hormone which tells the breasts to produce more milk. The amount of sucking the baby does therefore directly controls the amount of milk that is produced. When a mother wants to stop breast-feeding, she slowly cuts down the baby's sucking time and the amount of milk is gradually reduced.

Things a breast-feeding mother needs to do

In order to produce enough milk for the baby and satisfy the needs of her own body, a breast-feeding mother needs to eat plenty of nourishing food: breast-feeding uses between 600 and 800 extra calories a day. She also needs to drink plenty of liquid and to rest as much as possible.

The things a mother eats and drinks affect the content and taste of her milk. There is no food she definitely has to avoid, but certain foods may upset certain babies. Alcohol can pass into the milk but probably does no harm in small amounts. Nicotine, certain medicines and other drugs can also pass into the milk.

Bottle-feeding

For mothers who decide to bottle-feed their babies, preparing feeds and cleaning bottles and equipment can take up quite a lot of time. You might be able to help by doing this, or by actually giving the baby a bottle. You would have to get the baby's mother or father to show you exactly what to do, but you may find some useful tips and reminders here.

Fighting germs

A new baby's body has had no time to build up resistance to the germs which are all around us and generally do no harm to older people. Milk, especially warm milk, is an ideal breeding ground for germs. It is very important that everything that goes in young babies' mouths or touches their milk is sterile (free from germs). There are two methods of sterilizing feeding equipment. Whichever is used, the equipment must be absolutely clean before sterilizing begins.

1. You put the bottles, teats etc. in a steam sterilizer with a little water and switch on. The steam that is created sterilizes the equipment in about 10 minutes.

2. You soak the equipment in a chemical sterilizing solution. The chemicals come in the form of tablets, crystals or liquids to which you add water. To mix up the solution you follow the instructions on the packet. You usually have to soak things for at least half an hour before they are sterilized.

Here are some other important rules to help fight germs:
*Always wash your hands before handling a bottle or mixing up a feed.
*All water given to a baby in any form must first be boiled to make it sterile, then cooled.
* Once mixed, a feed must either be used immediately or stored in a fridge. Milk kept at room temperature breeds germs.

Milk and bottles

You cannot give babies ordinary cow's milk until they are about a year old, because it is too difficult for them to digest. There are many different brands of specially prepared milk for bottle-fed babies. Most are based on cow's milk which has been modified by various processes to make it as like human milk as possible. This is often referred to as "formula" milk and usually comes in powdered form.

Giving a feed

First, test the temperature of the milk by letting a few drops fall on the inside of your wrist. The milk should come at several drops a second and feel just warm. Babies prefer it at this temperature, though cold milk is not bad for them. If it is too cold, stand the bottle in a bowl of warm water; if it is too hot, stand it in the fridge.

Make yourself comfortable in a chair, with the baby cradled in one arm. The baby should be fairly upright, with her head well above her stomach. Support your arm with cushions, otherwise it will ache.

You could put a cloth around the baby's neck or have one handy, ready to mop up dribbles.

Formula milk has to be mixed with boiled water. Instructions about how to do this are given on each container. It is very important to follow them carefully and use exactly the right amount of powder. It is very bad for a baby to have too rich a mixture.

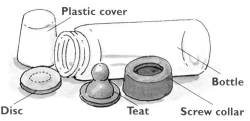

Plastic cover

Bottle

Disc   **Teat**   **Screw collar**

Most feeding bottles are made of glass or plastic and have a rubber teat which fits onto the bottle with a screw collar. There is also a plastic cover for the teat and a disc which you use under the collar, if you want to seal the bottle so that milk cannot leak out.

Touch the baby on the cheek that is nearer to you. She will turn her head toward you.

Touch her lips with the teat and she will take it into her mouth and start sucking. Make sure the teat goes well back in her mouth and keep the bottle tipped up so the teat is always full of milk, not air.

During the feed the teat may flatten and stop any more milk getting out. If this happens, pull it gently away from the side of the baby's mouth, so a little air can get into the bottle.

The baby may need little breaks during feeding. She will stop sucking and let go of the bottle. She may also need winding (see right). If you have winded her and she still does not want the bottle, she has probably had enough.

Wind

Most babies tend to swallow some air (wind) while they are feeding. This goes down to their stomachs with their milk and can make them feel uncomfortably full or give them pain. If this happens, they need to burp air up.

Milk is heavier than air. If you keep the baby in a fairly upright position, the air will rise above the milk and escape more easily.

To get wind up, all you need to do is hold the baby upright. If she does not burp after a minute or two, gently rub or pat her back. If she still does not burp, she may not have any wind.

Bringing up milk

If there is air below the milk in the baby's stomach, she may bring up a little milk when she burps. She may also bring up milk if she has swallowed more than she could comfortably hold. Babies often do this. It is nothing to worry about.

Hiccups

Babies often get hiccups, especially after feeding. It does not seem to bother them and does no harm.

Nappies

Changing a nappy is a very useful way of helping to look after a baby. A newborn baby needs to be changed about six to eight times a day and most babies continue to wear nappies until they are at least two years old. It is usual to change a nappy before or after each feed and whenever else you suspect it is dirty. Everyone tends to develop their own particular nappy-changing routine, so you will need to watch what a baby's parents normally do before attempting a change yourself. The information given here will then remind you what to do.

Different types of nappies

There are two main types of nappies: towelling, which you wash after each use, and disposable, which you throw away.

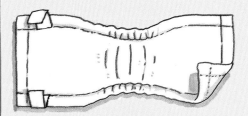 

Disposable nappies consist of absorbent padding backed by plastic. They usually have adhesive tabs with which to fasten them. There are many different brands of disposables and there are different shapes to fit girls and boys.

Washable nappies consist of either a triangle or square of towelling. Square nappies need folding before you use them. You fasten them with nappy pins (large safety pins with special safety hoods to stop them snapping open).

Changing a nappy

1 Before you start, check that you have everything you need within reach, so that you do not have to leave the baby while you find things. You will need:

1. A plastic covered *changing mat* or a *towel* on which to lay the baby.
2. Special *baby wipes*, or *cotton wool* and *baby lotion* or a small bowl of *warm water*, for cleaning the baby's bottom.
3. *Cream* to protect the baby's bottom.
4. A *clean nappy* plus *nappy liner* and *plastic pants*, if used. Make sure you fold a towelling nappy before you start and that you have nappy pins.
5. A *bucket*, bin or plastic bag for the dirty nappy.
6. A *clean set of clothes* in case the nappy has leaked.

You can lay the baby across your knees, but it is probably easier to lay him on a changing mat or folded towel on a flat surface in front of you. The floor is the safest place.

Undo the baby's nappy and lift his bottom in the air by holding both ankles in one hand with a finger between them. With the other hand, remove the dirty nappy.

Nappy liners

Nappy liners are squares of disposable material designed to be placed inside towelling nappies to stop them getting so dirty. There are also washable "one-way" nappy liners, which keep the baby's bottom drier by letting urine through one way but not back the other.

Plastic pants

Plastic pants are an extra that can be used with any type of nappy. Some have elasticated legs and waists and simply pull on. Others do up with poppers at the sides. Some are made of very soft plastic which you tie in a knot at both sides, or at the front and back.

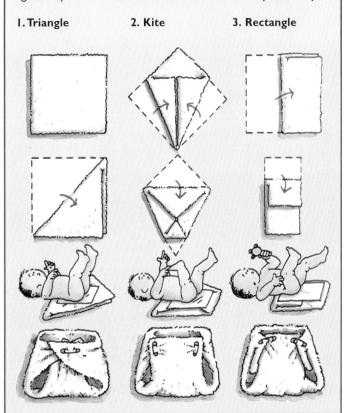

Three ways to fold a nappy

Different ways of folding nappies suit babies of different ages, shapes, sizes and sex. Here are three for you to try.

1. Triangle   2. Kite   3. Rectangle

4 Clean the baby's bottom thoroughly using baby wipes, or cotton wool and baby lotion or warm water. If you use water, make sure you dry the skin carefully afterward.

5 Put the clean nappy in position under the baby and then put some protective cream on his bottom. This helps to prevent moisture reaching his skin and giving him "nappy rash".

6 Bring the front part of the nappy up through the baby's legs and fasten it. With a disposable, be careful not to get cream on the sticky tabs as this will stop them sticking and you may have to add adhesive tape. With a towelling nappy, keep some of your fingers between the baby's skin and the nappy pin, when you fasten it, to make sure you do not prick the baby.

7 Wash your hands.

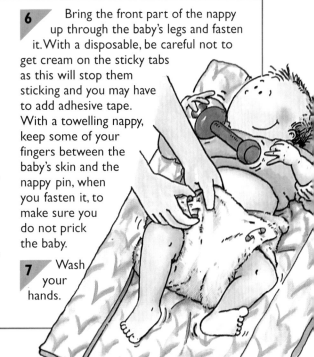

Growing and learning

Babies start life with very little control over their bodies, but during the first year or so they rapidly learn to move the different parts of their bodies at their own will. Their control develops from the head downward, ending with the legs and feet.

Different babies develop at very different rates and early development seems to bear little relation to ability later in life. The ages given in this section give only an indication of when each development may happen; there can be very wide variations. All babies, however, tend to go through the same stages and in the same order. If you know a baby, see if you can tell which stage she has reached in each of the sections below.

Learning to support head

At birth
When a baby is lifted up, his head flops because his neck muscles cannot support it. When lying on his front, he can lift his head just enough to turn his face to one side.

At 6 weeks
He can turn his head from side to side, when lying on his back. On his front, he can lift his head up for a few seconds.

At 3 months
He can lift his head and shoulders when lying on his front and hold his head steady when held upright.

At 6 months
He can lift his head when lying on his back.

Learning to use hands

At 3 months
A baby has "discovered" her hands. She plays with them and watches them, can briefly hold things placed in them, and starts reaching out to touch things.

At 6 months
She pats and strokes things, can reach out and grasp things in both hands and transfer things from one hand to the other.

At 7 months
She can pick things up with only one hand, holding her fingers and thumb together like a scoop. She may offer them to other people, but does not know how to let go of them.

At 9 months
She starts to gain control over each finger separately and points to things, using just one finger.

At 11 months
She learns to grip things between her fingers and thumb and can now pick up very small objects.

At 12 months
She learns to let go of things by deliberately uncurling her fingers.

Rolling over

At birth
A new baby's natural position is all curled up.

At 3 months
His body has straightened out. He learns to roll from his back to his side and back again.

At 4 months
He learns to roll from his front onto his back.

At 6 months
He learns to roll from his back to his front.

At 8 months
Some babies learn to move around by rolling over and over.

At birth
If you try to place a baby in a sitting position, her back curves forward and her head flops onto her knees.

At 6 weeks
She can be propped up in a sitting position by using cushions or a baby chair.

At 4 months
If you support her arms, she can hold a sitting position.

At 6 months
She can sit unsupported for a few seconds but her balance is bad. The bottom of her back is still curved.

At 7 months
She may put her hands on the floor to help her balance.

At 8 months
She can sit unsupported if she keeps still.

At 9 months
She can reach forward for toys and learns to twist around to reach things to the side or behind her. She may later start to move by shuffling along on her bottom.

At 12 months
She learns to lie down again by rolling over to one side and breaking her fall.

At 4 months
He can lift his head and shoulders by taking the weight on his arms and hands.

At 5 months
He raises both his chest and legs off the floor and makes swimming movements.

At 6 months
He bends his knees up under his body and gets into a crawling position.

At 8 months
He rocks backward and forward and swivels round but cannot actually move along.

At 9 months
He learns to coordinate his arm and leg movements to move himself along. Babies often move backward before they can move forward, because their arms are stronger and better coordinated than their legs.

At 6 months
She bounces up and down, by bending and straightening her legs when held upright with her feet touching a firm surface. She then starts to bounce from one foot to the other and later puts one foot in front of the other.

At 10 months
She can take her own weight on her feet by now but cannot balance. She uses furniture or people to pull herself from a sitting or kneeling to a standing position. At first she cannot sit down again without help.

At 11 months
She walks forward if her hands are held.

At 12 months
She walks sideways, holding onto furniture.

At 13 months
She stands unsupported and learns to walk a step between gaps in the furniture.

At 15 months
She walks fairly steadily for short distances.

41

Growing and changing shape

Although babies of the same age vary enormously in size and weight, the first two years of life are a time of very rapid growth for all babies. The speed and amount of growth depends largely on characteristics inherited from both parents.

During the first week of life, most babies lose weight, regaining their birth weight by the time they are 10 days old. A baby of average size weighs roughly twice his birth weight at six months old and three times his birth weight at the end of his first year.

A baby's height increases by approximately half during the first year. By the time a girl is 18 months old, she has reached roughly half her adult height. Boys reach half their adult height at about two years old.

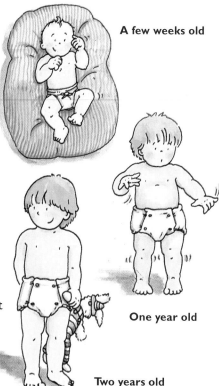

A few weeks old

One year old

Two years old

The proportions of the body change throughout childhood and adolescence, but the changes are especially noticeable during the first two years. During the first year, the head becomes a smaller proportion of the whole body, although it does increase in size very rapidly. The legs and arms get longer in proportion to the rest of the body. During the second year, the body elongates and looks firmer and more muscular.

Teeth

Most babies are born without any teeth showing through their gums. The first one often appears after about six months, but it is not unusual to wait a year before any teeth come through. Occasionally, a baby may be born with a tooth already visible. By the time they are three, most children have a full set. Sometimes, as a tooth pushes its way through the gum, it can be painful for the baby. This may make him miserable and irritable. It may also make him dribble and give him red, blotchy patches on his cheeks.

There are 20 teeth in the first, or "milk" set. (The second set consists of 32 teeth. It does not start appearing until a child is about six or seven.)

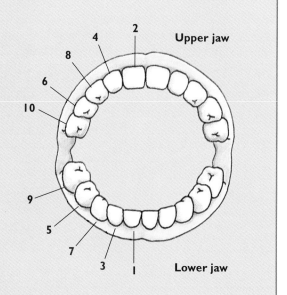

Upper jaw

Lower jaw

The teeth usually appear in the order shown here. Only half the set is numbered, because matching pairs from both sides of the mouth tend to appear at about the same time.

Playing and learning

Babies learn very rapidly during their first two years, and playing is one of their main ways of learning and trying out what they have learnt. When you play with them, give them plenty of time to take things in and react to them - they have much slower reactions than older children. Most babies have a short attention span, though they may enjoy some games so much that they want to play them over and over again. They need plenty of variety in the things they play with, but games with people and all sorts of ordinary household objects can entertain and teach them just as much as bought toys. Below are some play ideas, divided into four age categories.

0 to 3 months

People and things to look at and listen to. The more variety, the better.

3 to 6 months

Things to touch and hold - nothing too small as babies soon try to put everything into their mouths.

Things that make a noise when hit or shaken.

Bouncing on a knee or rolling on a soft surface.

6 to 12 months

Things that roll will encourage a baby to start moving after them.

Containers and things to put in them and take out again.

Soft toys

Bath toys

Looking in mirrors

Looking at pictures in books, magazines and brochures.

Hiding and finding games.

Bricks and things to build with.

12 months onward

Things to throw and kick.

Things to sort into groups.

Things to push along.

Things to pull along.

Things to fit together.

Things to fill and empty.

Things to make shapes with.

Games involving rhymes and actions.

43

Learning to talk

A baby starts to communicate with the people around her long before she can talk. She does this by her expressions and movements, by smiling (from about six weeks) and laughing (from about four months) and by using a great variety of sounds. The more you respond to her, the more she will want to communicate. Gradually, she starts to recognize certain sounds, realize they have a meaning and try to make them herself. She will probably understand a great many words before she can say anything at all herself. Below is a rough outline of the stages in learning to talk.

0 to 6 weeks   **At 6 weeks**
Cries.   **Gurgles**
Silently opens
and closes
mouth.

At 4 months
Makes cooing noises - at first long vowel sounds, later adds first consonants.

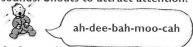

At 7 months
Starts making two-syllabled "babbling" sounds by repeating the first syllable.
At 8 months
Makes more and more complicated sounds. Shouts to attract attention.

ah-dee-bah-moo-cah

At 9 months
Joins up a variety of different sounds into "sentences". Tries out different intonation patterns.

dog ball dada

At 12 months
Uses first real words. These are nearly always labels for people or things. May make up own words. Over the next few months, slowly learns more words.
At 18 months
Starts learning new words more rapidly.

dog go   no ted   more dink

At 24 months
Starts linking words together to form simple sentences.

Becoming more independent

As babies gain more control over their own bodies and more understanding of the world around them, they start to become less dependent on other people and do more things for themselves. Below are two of the biggest steps toward independence that a small child makes.

1 Sometime between three and six months old, a baby starts to need more than just milk to satisfy his hunger. He can then have small tastes of a variety of everyday foods that have been mushed to a purée. The amounts are gradually increased until he is having solid food (not just milk) at every meal.

Soon he learns to chew food and can pick up things in his fingers and get them into his mouth. Then he starts to grab hold of the spoon and, a little later, manages to use it to put some food in his mouth. With constant practice he gets better and better at using the spoon, until he can feed himself a complete meal.

Sometime during the second year, a baby starts to be aware in advance when he is about to dirty or wet his nappy. Once he can give warning of this, he can be taught to sit on a potty instead. It can take him several months to learn to use the potty every time he needs it. When he knows how to use a potty, he can learn to use the toilet. He will need holding steady on the seat and help with undressing and dressing for some time.

Babysitter's guide

On this page and the next one are some questions to ask and safety tips to remember when you look after a baby or young child on your own. To make it easier for you, the information is divided into two sections: the first is about looking after babies who are not yet moving around by themselves; the second about looking after older babies and toddlers.

When you babysit, it is very important to think of everything you might want to know, and find out exactly what you are expected to do, before the parents leave.

Questions to ask (young babies)

Will she need to be given a bottle? If yes, should you give her juice, boiled water, or milk? Should it be warm or cold? What time should you give it? Get exact instructions about how to prepare milk.

Will she need a nappy change? Where are the nappies and changing equipment? What is the normal nappy-changing routine?

Is she likely to want to sleep? Does she have any comfort habits to help her get to sleep? Does she sleep on her back or her side?

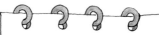

Telephone numbers

Always make sure you have:

1. The telephone number and address of the place where the parents are going.
2. The telephone number of the child's doctor.
3. The telephone number of an adult friend or relative who lives nearby.

Safety tips (young babies)

Never leave a baby alone with a bottle - she might choke.

Never give a baby a pillow to sleep on.

Don't put bouncy baby chairs on tables or sofas. They can sometimes move as they bounce and fall off.

Make sure that strong sunlight is not shining into the baby's face.

Don't leave a baby lying on a bed or table. Even if she cannot crawl, she may wriggle or roll off.

Hold the bannisters while you carry a baby up or down stairs. It is easy to trip and lose your balance.

Don't let toddlers pick the baby up.

If there is a cat in the house, make sure it does not get into the baby's cot. Cats like snuggling up in warm places, but might lie on top of the baby and smother her.

Be very careful to keep hot drinks away from a baby. A spill could be dangerous.

Watch that the baby does not put anything in her mouth.

Questions to ask (older babies)

When babies become more aware of what is going on around them, they usually need a little time to get to know a new babysitter before their parents leave. They also like to have everything done in exactly the way they are used to.

Do you need to give him any food or drink? Which cup, plate and spoon should you use? Does he need a bib? Which chair does he use?

Will you need to change a nappy, or help him to use the potty or toilet? What does he call the toilet?

What time does he go to bed? What is his normal bedtime routine? Does he have a comforter, or a favourite toy or book to take to bed? What should you do if he will not go to sleep, or wakes up crying?

Safety tips (older babies)

Do not leave a mobile baby alone in a room, unless he is in a cot.

When he climbs onto things, be ready to catch him if he falls off.

Beware that he does not put sharp things, or things that could choke him, into his mouth.

Watch him carefully on steps and stairs.

Do not let him play with plastic bags.

Watch out for things he might try to pull, such as the cord of an iron or kettle, or a tablecloth hanging within reach.

Keep knives, scissors, pins, needles, matches, glasses, mugs of hot drinks and full teapots well out of reach.

Keep him away from electric sockets and plugs, and hot fires, ovens, radiators and towel rails.

Toddlers may want to taste medicines and household cleaners. Make sure they do not get hold of any.

Never leave a baby or toddler alone in a high chair.

Never leave a baby or toddler alone in a bath, or playing with water in a bowl or sink.

Playing with doors can easily lead to trapped fingers and banged heads.

Glossary

Birth control. Prevention of sexual intercourse from leading to pregnancy.

Cells. The basic living units of which the body is composed.

Cervix. The lower end of the uterus, which opens to let the baby through during birth.

Conceive. Become pregnant.

Conception. The joining of a sperm cell and an egg cell. This is the start of a new individual.

Contraception. Birth control (see above).

Delivery. Labour; birth.

Embryo. A developing baby in the early stages of pregnancy.

Family planning. Contraception; birth control (see above).

Fertilization. Conception (see above).

Fetus. A developing baby between the 12th week and the end of pregnancy.

Gland. A group of cells which produces and releases substances which have an effect on another part of the body.

Hormones. Chemical substances which control certain processes in the body. They are produced in glands and are carried around the body in the blood.

Implantation. The embedding of a fertilized egg in the lining of the uterus.

Infertility. Inability to have children.

Labour. The process by which a baby leaves its mother's body; birth.

Menstrual period. Period (see below).

Ovary. Female sex gland which produces eggs. Each female has a pair of ovaries.

Ovulation. The release of an ovum from an ovary. In most women this happens about once a month.

Ovum (ova). Egg cell (egg cells).

Period. About two weeks after ovulation, the lining of a woman's uterus disintegrates and passes out of her body, unless a fertilized ovum has become implanted in it. The process of shedding the lining is called having a period.

Placenta. The organ which transfers food and oxygen from the mother to the baby in the uterus, and transfers the baby's waste products back to the mother.

Reproduction. Production of offspring.

Sperm. Male sex cells.

Testes. Testicles.

Umbilical cord. The cord which connects the baby and the placenta in the uterus.

Uterus. The stretchy bag inside a female, in which a baby grows during pregnancy.

Vagina. The tube which leads from the outside of a female's body to her uterus.

Womb. Uterus (see above).

Useful addresses

The following places can provide information and lists of recommended books and booklets about various aspects of sex, pregnancy, birth and childcare.

The Health Education Authority, Hamilton House, Mabledon Place, London WC1H 9TX

Relate Marriage Guidance, Herbert Gray College, Little Church Street, Rugby CV21 3AP

The Family Planning Association, 27 Mortimer Street, London W1A 4QW

The National Childbirth Trust, Alexandra House, Oldham Terrace, London W3 6NH

Index